GUEST BLOGGING GOLDMINE

GUEST
BLOGGING
GOLDMINE

*How I Got **More Than 100,000 Visitors** a Month on My Blog in 9 Months Using a Free Marketing Strategy, and Other Ways to **Earn Consistent Income** from Your Blog.*

TOM CORSON-KNOWLES

Published by TCK Publishing

www.TCKPublishing.com

To join my free step-by-step video training course on how to start a blog from scratch and turn it into a business come visit:

www.BlogBusinessSchool.com

Thank you for buying
Guest Blogging Goldmine

EARNINGS DISCLAIMER

When addressing financial matters in any of our books, sites, videos, newsletters or other content, we've taken every effort to ensure we accurately represent our products and services and their ability to improve your life or grow your business. However, there is no guarantee that you will get any results or earn any money using any of our ideas, tools, strategies or recommendations, and we do not purport any "get rich schemes" in any of our content. Nothing in this book is a promise or guarantee of earnings. Your level of success in attaining similar results is dependent upon a number of factors including your skill, knowledge, ability, dedication, business savvy, network, and financial situation, to name a few. Because these factors differ according to individuals, we cannot and do not guarantee your success, income level, or ability to earn revenue. You alone are responsible for your actions and results in life and business. Any forward-looking statements outlined in this book or on our Sites are simply our opinion and thus are not guarantees or promises for actual performance. It should be clear to you that by law we make no guarantees that you will achieve any results from our ideas or models presented in this book or on our Sites, and we offer no professional legal, medical, psychological or financial advice.

CONTENTS

WHY YOU SHOULD
READ THIS BOOK

I first started blogging in 2008. It was a completely frustrating and horrible experience for me. I hated it!

I wasted so hundreds of hours of work and thousands of dollars spent on marketing and advertising... with nothing to show for it!

I had very little traffic and no idea how to make money with the blog. I knew lots of other people were making money with their blogs, but why wasn't I?

I read about the founders of ProBlogger, Zen Habits, the Four Hour Work Week, and other big blogs who were earning six and seven-figure incomes just from blogging. How come I couldn't figure out how to earn just a few hundred dollars from my site?

And then, to make matters worse, I literally had nothing to show for all my hard work when Google shut down my first blog out of the blue – I lost everything! Every article I wrote, every post I created, the layout and design, all the hours invested and even the few hundred readers and subscribers I had... all gone overnight!

I took me 3 years to get back the confidence to start another blog again and try to turn it into a successful business, but I finally did it!

And that's what I want to share with you in this book: how to create a successful blog from scratch and turn it into a profitable business without having to make all the mistakes I did the first time around.

You see, blogging isn't just a way to express yourself or share your message; it's also a great way to earn an income and live the lifestyle of your dreams. Blogging opens you up to entirely new possibilities and opportunities for your life.

Personally, I've been able to earn a fabulous income and live my dream life here in Hawaii because of blogging. I've been able to meet some of the most influential people in the world and interview them personally because of my blog. I've received thousands of dollars in free books, free products, and free perks as a blogger. My blog helped launch my career as an international bestselling author.

It all started with a blog!

And it's not because I was born influential or rich. When I started blogging, no one knew who I was. All the success I've achieved is because blogging gives you the power to communicate with millions of people and make a huge difference in the world (and earn a lot of money if you do it right).

I want to share that power with you and show you exactly how to blog successfully so that you don't have to waste three years and tens of thousands of dollars like I did.

Let this book be your guide to becoming a successful blogger.

To your success,

Tom Corson-Knowles

CHAPTER 1

HOW TO CREATE YOUR OWN SELF-HOSTED WORDPRESS BLOG IN 30 MINUTES

When I created my first blog, I set it up all wrong, and that one little mistake cost me thousands of dollars and hundreds of hours of wasted time.

Set up your blog right from the beginning to avoid wasting money and time and missing out on big opportunities.

My first blog was hosted on Blogger's platform, which means I didn't have control of it – Google did. That was a huge mistake! Google shut down my blog a few months after I started and I lost everything.

Then I switched to a blog hosted on Wordpress.com – another big mistake! I guess I didn't learn the first time that if someone else owns my blog, that means I don't own it and I can't earn real money from it.

Finally, after a lot of testing, I found the best way to set up a blog using my a domain that I own and my own hosting, combined with the Wordpress blogging platform.

I've created a free training video for you that will show you exactly how to set up your own blog that you own using your own domain and hosting so that you can maximize your revenue and have complete control of your site.

You can watch the video trainings for free at:

www.BlogBusinessSchool.com

Why don't I just tell you in writing how to do it? Because it will just confuse you! The video tutorial shows you everything you need to do step by step so you don't have to waste any time. Your blog will be set up in just a few minutes after you watch the video.

In the videos, you'll see me on my computer going to the right websites, clicking the buttons in the right place, and you can literally just watch and follow along as you learn how to build your own high quality, professional website in just a few minutes. No experience or technical skills required!

Obviously, if you already have your own self-hosted Wordpress blog, you won't need to watch that tutorial, but you might find the other videos on getting traffic and outsourcing very helpful when it comes to growing your blogging business.

CHAPTER 2

TRAFFIC:
THE SCIENCE OF GETTING
BLOG READERS
AND PAYING CUSTOMERS

Traffic is what makes or breaks you as a blogger. You can write anything you want, but if you have no readers how big of an impact will your words make?

Who will take action based on what you wrote?

Who will be inspired, uplifted and educated by your words?

Who will buy from you?

No one!

...until you get the traffic.

You see, traffic is what stops most bloggers from truly making a difference in the world (and a profit). Without traffic, it's like you're shouting your message in the middle of the woods, and no one can hear you but yourself.

But once you start getting high quality traffic, you can reach the entire world. Readers will get your message and they will share it with their friends and on social networks and it will spread.

So how do you get traffic?

THE FASTEST, EASIEST, MOST POWERFUL WAY TO GET TRAFFIC

The fastest, most effective, easiest and cheapest way to grow your blog, increase your traffic, and improve your search engine rankings is by guest blogging and/or soliciting links from other bloggers.

Now, almost everyone in the internet world has heard of guest blogging - but *very few* people actually use this strategy effectively and efficiently.

I'm going to show you how to use this strategy to build hundreds of high quality links to your site and funnel thousands of visitors from other blogs in your niche to your blog.

The difference between someone who's successful as a guest blogger and someone who's not, can be summed up by three key principles of success:

Blogging Success Principle 1

The successful person has persistence and will continue to actively write guest articles month after month.

Blogging Success Principle 2

The successful person has the right knowledge and understands how to contact bloggers in order to get a high rate of response.

Blogging Success Principle 3

The successful person understands which blogs have the most link value and which blogs to avoid (such as spam blogs that have zero link value, of which sadly there are millions today).

In this book, you're going to learn everything you need to know about how to successfully implement guest blogging and use it to create a highway of steady traffic to your site.

Ready?

THE GUEST BLOGGING SYSTEM

VERY IMPORTANT NOTE: This is a streamlined process for contacting other blog owners and building a relationship with them that will hopefully lead to you posting a guest article on their site in exchange for a link to yours (usually this link will appear in the "Bio" section at the bottom of the article).

As with any streamlined process for contacting and communicating with people, there is a thin line between spamming and real genuine communication.

Please, DO NOT use this system to spam bloggers. We bloggers get enough spam as it is, and I am not recommending that anyone make the spam problem any worse.

Keep your messages honest, helpful, genuine and spam-free. We do NOT need more spammers out there, but we're in desperate need of more bloggers who really get it and want to add value. I hope you get it!

ANOTHER NOTE ABOUT GUEST BLOGGING:

You better have at least 10 posts on your blog before even attempting to implement this guest blogging system. Other serious bloggers want to make sure you're serious before they are going to invest the time or energy in promoting your articles to their readers.

If you don't have enough posts yet, just go to work on writing more posts for your own site, and then apply this system afterwards. If you apply it with only 1 or 2 blog posts on your site, you will get a very poor response from other bloggers simply because your blog seems so empty without any helpful and interesting content for your readers.

Add some great content to your own site before you try to write content for other sites in your niche.

STEP 1. PREPARATION

In order to quickly and effectively implement this system, you're going to need:

The Alexa/PageRank plugins for your web browser- (I use Google Chrome, but whatever browser you use there will be a plugin to download that allows you to see the Alexa rankings of websites you're looking at, as well as their Google PageRank, right in your browser).

If you're using Google Chrome, just search "Google Chrome Alexa plugin" and download and install it.

If you're using Internet Explorer, just search "Internet Explorer Alexa plugin" and download and install it.

If you're using Mozilla Firefox, just search "Mozilla Firefox Alexa plugin" and download and install it.

If you're using Safari, just search "Safari Alexa plugin" and download and install it.

Next, adjust your Google search settings to list the first 100 search results, not the standard 10 results. This is going to save you a lot of time and clicks later on as you're browsing for high traffic blogs in your field.

Here's how to change your search results in Google:

Step 1:   Go to www.Google.com

Step 2:   Type in your search (any search will do) and hit enter

Step 3:   Click the upper right button that looks like a mechanical gear or a star

Step 4: Click on "Search Settings"

Step 5: In the "Results Per Page" section, scroll it from 10 results per page to 100 results per page.

Congratulations! Now you're ready to start searching for blogs that will post your guest articles and link back to your site.

STEP 2. SEARCHING FOR THE RIGHT BLOGS

You want to search for other blogs in your niche, or in niches that are similar or compatible with yours so that you can build a relationship with them and share your valuable information with their audience.

For example, if you have a blog about dog training, you could search for blogs about dogs, or blogs about dog training, or blogs about cats and cat training (you could write an article for them about dogs vs. cats - the never-ending debate!)

The key here is to think of as many different types of niches that you could write about and add value to. The more value you add, the more traffic you will get.

Just remember to be open-minded. Maybe horse-training blogs would like you to write an article for them about the top 5 things you learned as a dog trainer and how that could be applied to training horses. Be creative and you will find many more opportunities for collaboration, guest blogging and building links to your site.

Note: Many SEO gurus out there believe that ONLY links from SIMILAR websites to your site are useful in helping you get more targeted traffic from search engines.

I do not agree with this common sentiment. Any website that has a) high quality content, b) high quality incoming links and c) high quality outgoing links will provide very valuable "link juice" to your site should they decide to link to you, regardless of the topic of the website. Just avoid sites that promote illegal activities, guns, hate speech or pornography, or sites with little or no unique content or inbound links.

Once you've picked your search term (let's say it's "dog training" for now), you're going to add blog to the end of that term.

So you would go to Google.com, type in "dog training blog" and hit search!

STEP 3. CLICK AND ANALYZE

At first, this step will take you a bit of time because you're just starting to learn how blogs work and how to navigate quickly through all sites and all the data.

Here are some general tips to make figuring out which sites to contact and which sites to ignore a whole lot easier:

First, if it's a news site, throw it out.

For example, if you see well.blogs.newyorktimes.com in the search results, just skip past it, because I don't think the New York Times is going to accept your guest post when you're just starting out.

Second, if you see the same domain more than once, only click one of them.

Sometimes, Google will give you the same domain name several times in a search, so just click one of them and skip the extras.

For example, you may see the following sites in the search results:

> well.blogs.nytimes.com
>
> business.blogs.nytimes.com
>
> science.blogs.nytimes.com

If you see search results with several links from one domain there's no reason to click all of those links from the same website so just click one of them and move down the list until you find a link to a new domain.

Third, ignore spam blogs and low quality sites!

Here's a good example:

This site has a Google PageRank 2, and most bloggers might think that means it's a great site to get a link from. But it's not!

The site has an Alexa rank of 15041954. That means there are more than 15 million sites getting more traffic than that site. In other words, the site is getting almost no traffic from Google or anyone else, so don't bother trying to get a link from a site like that because it won't do you any good.

Do no solicit sites like this for links. Even if you got a link from that site, it would do you more harm than good because it's quite likely Google has penalized that site for spamming, selling links, duplicate content or some other black-hat tricks.

If the Alexa rank alone wasn't enough to let you know that site was not worth contacting just look at the home page! It says it's a weight loss blog, but the home page article is just a spam advertisement for a "Coverking Stormproof Car" filled with affiliate links and ads!

If you see a site like this, close it out immediately and move on! (*Also, if you get contacted by someone offering to sell or trade links from a site like that, just ignore them.*)

Don't do business with spammers. It will do more harm than good and could destroy your precious reputation with Google, especially when your site is new.

AN IMPORTANT NOTE

I want to reiterate a very important point here...

Your mission is to become a successful blogger. If you want to achieve that mission, then you must associate with other bloggers who have good ethics, high quality content and high quality links.

Do NOT associate with any website in any way that has spam, sells links, buys links, or uses black hat SEO... because if you do, it will come to bite you in the butt! Be careful whom you hang around with. And, on the internet, be careful what sites you ask to link to you and what sites you link to. It's just good business.

WHAT YOU'RE LOOKING FOR IN A GOOD BLOG

You're basically looking for quality sites with 1) unique content that 2) get lots of traffic and 3) are recognized by Google as being a legitimate, authoritative site.

Here are my general rules:

PAGERANK

The PageRank should be 1 or higher. When you're starting out, it's fine to guest post on lots of PR 1 or PR2 websites. As your blog grows in traffic, you may not have time to write for such sites and would want to write for PR 3 or higher sites (but it may take you a few months get to that point so be patient!)

WHAT IS GOOGLE PAGERANK?

Google PageRank is an indicator from 0 to 10 that tells you how much Google values a website in terms of its "authority." A site with a PageRank 0 has basically no authority (either because it's brand new or because it has no quality incoming links).

A site with a PageRank 10 has extremely high authority, and there are very few of them. Google and Twitter have PageRank 10. Facebook has a PageRank 9.

Contrary to what many SEO gurus will tell you, PageRank cannot tell you whether or not a site is worth getting a link from. Google now uses PageRank to "fool" SEO experts into thinking Google actually uses PageRank to determine search engine results – they don't!

For example, the spam site I showed you before, with a PageRank 2 would not be worth getting a link from. In fact, if you had hundreds of links from sites like that, Google might penalize your site or even blacklist it.

This is why I only use PageRank as a general guide to whether or not a site is worth getting a link from. I recommend you use other factors like the Alexa rank and the site's design and content to guide you as well.

ALEXA RANK

When you first start out, any site with an Alexa rank of 1,000,000 or lower should be just fine for guest posting. Basically, if a site is in the top 1 million sites, it's probably a decent site (just make sure the site

LOOKS like a legitimate website too and is not really a spam site like the example above).

WHAT IS ALEXA RANK?

Alexa is an independent website that monitors all the sites on the internet and ranks them in terms of their monthly, weekly and daily traffic and page views.

The Alexa rank starts at 1 for the website with the most traffic in the world (currently Facebook) and counts up from there. Therefore, the lower your site's Alexa rank, the better.

I use the Alexa rank in conjunction with Google PageRank to make sure a site is legitimate and worthy of guest posting. For example, if a site has a Google PageRank 5 (a very nice, high PageRank) and an Alexa rank of 12,231,221 (a very poor Alexa rank), then I know something is amiss – it doesn't add up.

I would never solicit a link from a site like that because they are obviously using some kind of black-hat SEO techniques or they have been penalized by Google – either way, I want nothing to do with a site like that. And neither should you!

Ideally, you want to write guest posts for blogs that have both a high PageRank (2 or higher) and a low Alexa rank (200,000 or less). When you're first starting out, you may have to settle for writing on smaller sites until you can work your way up to writing exclusively for bigger sites.

SITE LAYOUT AND CONTENT

The site needs to look like it was designed by a human, for people to actually read. If the only thing you see above the fold is AdSense ads in the header and sidebar, then it's probably a spam site. If it looks like a cookie-cutter website with no human elements to it, it's probably just junk.

If the site's domain is something like www.weightlossdieting.com but you actually look at the site and all the articles are about electronics, then it's probably a spam site. You want to make sure the site is "congruent" and that it actually looks like a legitimate website with useful information, and that it's actively being managed by a real person.

Remember, you're looking for a site that looks like a **real person** actually manages it.

The Alexa rank, Google PageRank, site design and content need to all be telling the same story – that this is a legitimate website with helpful information that gets a good amount of visitors on a daily basis. Otherwise, it's not worth getting a link from. Period.

QUESTIONABLE CONTENT

It pretty much goes without saying that you should avoid any sites that contain pornography, hate speech, illegal activities or anything that might shine a poor light on you and your business. Don't get caught up in trying to get links and forget that it's about *quality first* and quantity second!

Getting links from questionable sites will only hurt your traffic not help it.

Remember this before you ever hire someone else to build links to your website!

Make sure you are reviewing the work they're doing and that they're not just sending spam links to your website. Many so-called SEO experts can do more harm than good when it comes to getting traffic to your site.

A handful of high quality links are **far more valuable** than hundreds or thousands of low-quality links.

STEP 4. CONTACTING BLOGGERS

If the site passes your PageRank an Alexa rank check, and looks like a real quality site written by a real human for real people to read, it's time to contact them.

You may be surprised, but you will find many bloggers who have no way to contact them through their blog because they haven't listed their email address anywhere, there's no web form for contacting them, or there's no "Contact Page."

It's almost as if they don't want anyone to contact them!

I just move on when I find a blog like this, because if you can't find a way to contact them, chances are they aren't serious enough about blogging to be worth contacting, even if you could figure out a way to find them.

Most often, sites like this are free blogs hosted on Blogger or Wordpress (the URL ends with a blogger or Wordpress such as www.example.blogger.com or www.example.Wordpress.com).

Helpful Tip: If you can't find a way to contact a blogger after being on their site for three minutes, it's probably not worth contacting them anyway.

There are 3 main ways a blogger will post their contact information:

CONTACT

They will have a web page called Contact or Contact Us - just use your keyboard to search for "contact."

Neat Trick: How to Find Text Anywhere on a Web Page

On a PC you can press CTRL + F and type in the word you're searching for.

On a Mac, hit the Apple Command Button + F and type what you're searching for.

Either way, your computer will automatically find the letters or words you typed into the search box if they exist on the page. If the text you're searching for appears multiple times on the page, you can press enter to scroll through and see the different places on the page where the text appears.

If you don't see a contact page or form, then try to find the...

ABOUT / ABOUT ME PAGE

Many times bloggers will have all their contact info in the About, About Me, or About Us page of their site.

Just use that nifty search trick I taught you before and type in "about". If you don't see that, then try to find their contact info in the...

SIDEBAR

Sometimes a blogger will list their contact info in the sidebar - so just look for it there if you can't find it elsewhere.

If that doesn't work, your last hope is...

SOCIAL MEDIA

Some bloggers, either because they're tired of being spammed or they just don't know better, will only have their contact info for Twitter, a Facebook Fan Page or other social media accounts.

You can send them a tweet or message on the social network and see if they respond!

If that doesn't work then it's time to...

MOVE ON

If you can't find a way to contact them using one of the four options mentioned before, then it's time to move on.

There are plenty of other high quality bloggers who actually care enough about their blog readers to provide their contact info. These are the bloggers you want to work with.

STEP 5. FOLLOW THROUGH

When a blog owner responds to your message, follow through.

If they ask you to write an article, write it promptly and send it to them. Make sure it meets their guidelines and specifications. Make sure it's a helpful article and not just promoting your blog. It should add real value to anyone who reads it. Make sure to edit your article so that it's not full of typos or grammatical errors.

In other words, do your best work, do it on time, and do what you say you're going to do. Make it easy to do business with you.

You can do all the promotion you want of your own blog and your work in your author bio beneath the guest post.

SEE GUEST POSTING IN ACTION

You can see one of my guest posts in action to get a feel for what they look like. Example Guest Post:

> http://ediblegoddess.com/2012/05/growing-
> your-own-fresh-produce-got-easier/

In this post, my author bio appears before the article begins (although most bloggers put the author bio underneath it).

Here's another example guest post where my author bio appears below the post along with a link to my websites:

> http://www.healmyptsd.com/2012/03/ptsd-
> nutrition-and-brain-repair.html

Now that you understand how the guest blogging process works and are contacting bloggers in your field, it's time to learn how to build relationships with these bloggers.

SAMPLE EMAIL TO BLOGGER

If you're not sure what to write to a blogger for a first-time contact, try something similar to this:

> *"Hi [First Name],*
>
> *I love your blog! It's always inspiring to see others like you who are sharing the message of [Your Niche] in an easy to understand and exciting way.*
>
> *I'd love to see if there's some way we could collaborate with our sites through guest blogging,*

social media, or something else. I blog about [Your Niche] too. Check it out and let me know if you think it's a good fit.

[Link To Your Site]

[Salutation],

[Your Name]"

I always like to keep my emails short, sweet and to the point and customize them to the blogger I'm contacting. For example, if I notice an article on their site about their two adorable poodles, I might say "I love poodles too!" or something similar to let them know you actually read their blog.

WHAT NOT TO DO

Here's an actual email sent to me by some spammer. Don't write like this.

Honestly, if you can't even write an email with good grammar and spelling how could you possibly write a good guest post for someone?

HORRIBLY WRITTEN EMAIL WHICH YOU SHOULD NEVER EMULATE

"Hi,

I saw your blog it is interesting, I want to introduce myself as a guest blogger. I have some interesting topics and contents are written by me after a short research..

If you are interested let me know...Looking forward to write useful contents for your blog..

Regards,

John"

Thanks John! I'll be sure to let you know when I need more random, poorly written articles with lots of typos and grammatical errors for my blog.

STEP 6. CONTINUE THE RELATIONSHIP

After you write a guest post for their site, you could ask if they'd like to write a post for your site. Offer to help them in return.

Another great thing you should do when you guest post is to share the article you wrote in all of your social media channels. Doing this helps promote their blog, and it helps you too by showing your fans and followers that you're a credible authority, worthy of your articles being posted on other sites and blogs.

Always be creative and open to more ways to collaborate with other bloggers and website owners. We all win when we help each other and work together.

Don't just be a taker. Be a giver too! Givers truly gain in the world of blogging.

MORE CONSISTENCY = MORE TRAFFIC

When it comes to blogging, more consistency will bring you more traffic.

One of the big mistakes new bloggers make is not being consistent. One month they write 20 blog posts and then they quit.

So the readers look at the blog and see that nothing new has been posted for weeks, so why even bother to subscribe? Why would someone want to follow a dead blog?

That's why consistency is so important! It lets your readers know you're a serious blogger and that you will continue to post information that is useful and helpful for them.

That's why I highly recommend creating a publication schedule for your blog. Publish a minimum of one post a week and stick to it. Always be consistent with your blogging.

I've never seen a rich blogger who wasn't consistently writing new posts.

CHAPTER 3

THREE DIFFERENT TYPES
OF BLOGGERS

There are 3 different types of blogs: small, medium and big blogs. Each of them functions very differently, and the bloggers that run them think very differently as well.

When you're contacting other bloggers, you need to make sure you understand which kind of blogger you're talking to – small, medium or big – and tailor your message to make sure you connect with them appropriately.

Let's talk about how to recognize what kind of blogger you're dealing with and how to approach these different types of bloggers to build a mutually beneficial relationship. Remember, it's all about win-win relationships. If it's not good for the blogger, they won't accept your guest post.

1. SMALL BLOGS

Small blogs are generally PageRank 2 or less and usually get less than 1,000 visitors a day to their site. They might have an Alexa rank of 400,000 or higher. When you first start out with your own blog, this is your realm – and these are the bloggers you will be working with first. And many of them will want to work with you – because you're in the same boat at the same time.

It's important when you're contacting small bloggers that you understand a few things:

Some small bloggers are not very serious about blogging. They may have just decided to start a blog on a whim without any real commitment, so they may not have even listed their contact info on their site. Furthermore, they may have become discouraged and quit blogging altogether.

Make sure you check their site to see if they've posted anything recently. If the last post you see is from several years ago, just move on, because they're not actively blogging (on that site) anymore. To succeed as a guest blogger, you'll have to learn how to avoid sites that aren't worth your time pursuing, and that means weeding out bloggers who aren't serious about marketing and promoting their site.

Small bloggers rarely get contacted by other bloggers and rarely get asked by someone like you to write a guest article for their site, so most small bloggers are flattered when you genuinely reach out to them asking to collaborate. This is great for you because it's these small bloggers who will be crucial to your early success as a blogger.

If you post guest articles on 20-30 high quality small blogs with a link back to your blog, you will become one of the larger small bloggers in your niche, almost on the verge of becoming a medium blog. Google will quickly recognize you as a reputable blogger with that many links from other small blogs.

2. MEDIUM BLOGS

Medium blogs generally get more than 1,000 visitors a day and are usually PageRank 3, 4 or 5. A medium blog might get up to 5,000 or even 10,000 visitors a day. A medium blog will be most likely be generating decent revenue from advertisements, affiliate sales and sponsorships. Some medium bloggers make a decent living blogging while others are just scraping by.

Even a few medium bloggers might make no income at all from their site because they don't know how and they structured it wrong, building their site on a Wordpress or blogger domain (such as example.blogger.com or example.Wordpress.com).

In general, medium bloggers are usually passionate about their blog and always looking for ways to improve. This is your key to approaching a medium blogger – helping them improve their blog and improve their standing and traffic online.

Medium bloggers often accept guest blog posts because there's just not enough time in the day to generate enough new content to keep their blog buzzing. You could be the answer to their prayers!

When you contact a medium blogger, you will want to make sure you personalize your message to them to let them know you have actually read their blog and actually care about them and their mission. Medium bloggers get enough traffic so they receive spam, probably daily, from people who want to get links from their site in one way or another.

You need to stand out from the competition by writing a relevant, genuine message that will connect with them. Show them how you can add value to their blog by providing high quality content for their readers.

If you have some really great relevant articles on your own blog, you can link to them as examples of your work. If you have some nice stats (like your site gets 700 visitors a day) to share with them, that also can make you more credible. But generally a medium blogger won't care about that. They just want to know that you're an expert who can add value to them by writing a great guest post, and maybe by promoting your guest post on social media as well.

3. BIG BLOGS

Big blogs are in a totally unique position. Big blogs generally get over 10,000 visitors a day. Many of them get 50,000 to 100,000 visitors a day or more. Blogs like TechCrunch, Engadget, Gizmodo, The Verge, and others receive a massive amount of traffic and they are not small blogging operations (anymore.) They are small to medium sized blogging companies. This means they don't use have one blogger who's in charge of calling the shots.

Big blogs are generally PR 6 or higher and have an Alexa rank of 5,000 or less.

Big blogs often have a business structure something like this:

> One owner (or a few partners), who started the blog who may, or may not participate in the day-to-day management anymore.
>
> Many writers (5, 10, or even hundreds of writers, who are freelance or part-time).
>
> A full-time editor who's in charge of scheduling publications, editing all the articles and making sure it fits their needs and style of blogging.
>
> An advertising/PR manager who manages inquiries about advertising on the blog as well as media inquiries (sometimes these functions are split between two people).

This is just the basic structure. Obviously every blog will be unique in their own way. But this new structure makes dealing with a big blog much different than dealing with a small or medium blogger.

If you want to write a guest post for one of these big blogs (which will get you massive traffic and very high quality links), then you need to make sure you really understand them first.

This is why you always must do research before you even consider contacting a big blog.

RESEARCHING A BIG BLOG

When you first find a big blog in your niche that you would like to get a link from, don't just contact them right away like you would with a small blogger. I highly recommend reading their blog for at least one hour. Read as many articles as you can, click as many pages as you can. Pay special attention to their "About Us" section, "Contact Us" section, and any pages related to hiring writers or accepting guest posts or inquiries.

What you want to do with this research is answer these questions:

1. WHAT IS THE BLOG ABOUT?

You need to know what the blog is about, and not just in vague terms such as "technology." You need to know what kind of posts they post most often, which posts get the most traffic, and what the About page says about what they do and why they do it. What makes them tick? What are their goals? What's their vision or purpose? How can you help them achieve that?

2. HOW LONG ARE THE AVERAGE BLOG POSTS?

This information will help you know how long you need to write your article for their site. Some sites only want very, very short articles (250-300 words), most sites want mid-size articles (500-600 words) and a few sites want very long articles (1,000+ words).

3. ARE THERE GUEST POSTS ON THE BLOG?

If the site does not have a single guest post on it yet, there might be a reason; the blogger might just not accept guest posts for whatever reason. If that's the case, save yourself time and move on to researching another site.

4. WHAT KIND OF GUEST POSTS ARE THERE? (WHAT TOPICS ARE COVERED AND WHO WERE THE GUEST AUTHORS?)

This info will help you come up with ideas for potential guest articles.

5. WHO'S THE EDITOR? WHO SHOULD I CONTACT ABOUT GUEST BLOGGING?

Know the contact person to sending articles to and with whom you are building a relationship.

6. WHAT KIND OF STORY ANGLE WOULD WORK BEST FOR THEM?

Use the info you've gathered to come up with 1 or 2 potential article angles.

Once you ask these questions, then you're ready to start planning your strategy. You need to find a story that will interest that blog enough for them to respond to your email and want to find out more. It's not like they're going to take your article and instantly publish it; they will want to ask questions and learn more about it most of the time. Your goal with a big blog is to start a relationship, not get just one guest post published.

Honestly, you will probably get rejected most of the time when you contact a big blog. The key is 1) focusing on the relationship and 2) being pleasantly persistent. Continue sending them relevant, useful information that they will want to use in an article.

Trust me, persistence pays off when dealing with these huge blogs, because just one mention could send you thousands or tens of thousands of highly targeted visitors to your site as well as provide you with a PR 6, 7, 8 or 9 link that is worth pure gold. A single link from a huge blog could be worth dozens, hundreds or even thousands of links from small or medium-sized blogs.

A SHORTCUT TO GETTING LINKS FROM BIG BLOGS

There is a shortcut to getting links from big blogs for those of you who are persistent, creative and tenacious.

First, sign up for helpareporter.com (HARO). HARO is a free service that connects journalists with expert sources. You could be the source for the next story on one of the big blogs.

Every day, you will get an email from HARO with leads from journalists who are looking for stories. If you see a writer from a big blog or freelance writer who publishes for big blogs, respond to their request with some very helpful information and you just might find yourself published on the big blogs with a link back to your site. Many big blogs already have guest posters or freelance writers. If you can help one of these writers when they're working on an article, you just might find yourself featured on the major blog with a link to your site.

That's exactly how I was featured in this article on American Express Open Forum about Twitter.

www.openforum.com/articles/getting-started-
with-twitter-ads

CHAPTER 4

MONETIZING YOUR BLOG

Now that you've built your blog, started posting great content, and know how to get traffic through guest blogging, it's time to learn how to monetize your blog so that you can make money from your work and create a sustainable business instead of just a hobby.

Here are the many ways you can monetize your blog.

1. ADS

Ads are the most common way to monetize a blog and should definitely be considered.

Here are some of the most common types of blog ads:

IN-TEXT ADS

Text link ads are ads that appear randomly throughout the text on your website, targeting specific keywords for advertisers and turning those words into text links which then pop-up with more information about the advertiser if the user scrolls over them. These ads can be a great way to monetize your site because they are not intrusive and the CPC (cost per click) of these ads can be very profitable for web publishers like yourself.

A good source for In-Text Ads is Infolinks[1]. I use them and it's a nice additional income.

TEXT LINK ADS

Text ads are just plain text links, often using a site's targeted keyword for the anchor text. For example, if I had a diet pill website, I might want to buy a text link from your blog with the anchor text "buy diet pills."

Technically, it is against Google's Terms of Service to buy and sell text ads because it's illegal to "sell links." Even so, this practice is still widely used by many bloggers and advertisers who focus on search engine traffic.

Personally, I don't recommend buying or selling text ads because you run the risk of having Google penalize your site. If you do decide to sell text ads, just make sure you only sell a few (I'd say no more than 4), and that you only link to reputable sites.

---

[1]   http://publishers.infolinks.com/signup.html?aid=1023419

DISPLAY ADS

Display ads are what most people think of when they think of website ads. They include graphical banner ads, leader boards, skyscrapers, large boxes and other sizes of graphical ads (a common one for bloggers is the 120x120 square ads).

Display ads are probably the most common type of ad and will result in your highest CPM (cost per mil, it's an industry term that means "price per thousand impressions," so if your CPM for a particular ad is $5, you will earn $5 every time that ad is loaded on your page 1,000 times).

Google AdSense[2] is a great program for Display ads.

POP-UP ADS

Pop-up ads are those annoying little things that pop up on the screen and ask you to buy something or "click here!" Pop-ups can be a great way to monetize your site, but I prefer to use pop-ups sparingly.

I personally prefer to use pop-ups with an opt-in form to my own email list so that I can build my list of potential customers and market to them over the long-term instead of selling pop-up ads.

---

[2] https://www.google.com/adsense

FLASH / DHTML ADS

Flash ads are animated banner ads. You might see the colors change or images move to catch your attention. They were basically invented because people became "banner blind" and started to ignore most banner ads. It's pretty hard to ignore most flash ads.

INTERSTITIAL ADS

Interstitial ads are full-page ads that appear between two webpages on a site.

For example, if a reader is on your home page and then clicks to read another article, the interstitial ad would pop-up before that user saw the second page. The user then has to either wait or click a button that says "continue to the next page" to get rid of the ad.

Personally, I don't like interstitial ads because they interfere with your readers' navigation and it wastes their time, regardless of their interest in the ad. I want to treat my readers well so that they spend more time on my site, not less.

VIDEO ADS

Video ads are videos that play, usually similar to a banner ad in their positioning and size.

Video ads can auto-play or wait until the user clicks them to play. I greatly prefer manual play video ads because they don't interfere with the readers browsing the way auto-play videos do.

ON-SITE SPONSORSHIP ADS

These are basically logos of companies that have sponsored your website. Many nonprofit groups use ads like this.

HOW TO FIND ADVERTISERS FOR YOUR SITE

You can contact advertisers directly for your site, but most bloggers will start by using an ad or media network because it saves a lot of time and is much more convenient.

AD NETWORKS

These include Google AdSense, AdBrite, Chitika, Infolinks, etc. These are a great way to monetize your blog through ads. Generally, these ads are either banner ads or text ads or link ads within your content itself. Each ad network has very different rules, policies and payouts so do your research.

Generally, AdSense is the best in terms of revenue generation followed by AdBrite and Infolinks (depending on your content).

MEDIA NETWORKS

Media networks like GLAM Media and others are very similar to ad networks except they require a few extra things from you. First, you must sign over your COMScore "Traffic Rights" to the ad network. Basically, this allows the media network to say that they have a network of 80 Million page views a month with part of that number being the page views from your site.

This is good for you because it helps them negotiate better ad deals, so it's a win-win if you decide to join a media network. Never sign an agreement for more than 1 year. One year is a long time in the internet business, and you don't want to get locked into a long term agreement if ad pricing changes or a better opportunity comes along.

MY BLOG ADVERTISING STRATEGY

I believe the value of a blog comes from its helpfulness to readers and its ease of navigation and access to valuable information. Because of this, I find ads that interrupt the reader or waste their time directly reduce the value of my site. Yes, you will get paid for those ad impressions, but I don't believe the payment is nearly worth the cost.

My ad strategy is to put as many ads on my website as a possibly can (to maximize ad revenue) while making these ads as unobtrusive as possible for my site's readers.

Generally, my favorite ads to use that are the least intrusive are: display ads, video ads (manually playing), text link ads, and on-site sponsorship ads. I find that a good combination of these various ad types produces great revenue for the site without harming the user experience.

As always, since it's your blog, it's your choice which ads to use.

2. AFFILIATE SALES

Affiliate sales can be a huge moneymaker as a blogger if you do it well.

If you've never heard of affiliate marketing, it's basically where you promote someone else's product or service, and they pay you a commission for every sale.

Every affiliate program is unique and different, but the industry standard for most digital products (ebooks, video training courses, seminars, etc.) is usually 50%, but the range is generally from 25%-75% for digital products.

Physical products usually offer much lower commission percentages because of the cost of delivering and manufacturing the product, so the range could be 2%-50% on a physical product. It all depends on the merchant (the person or company that created the product).

Some products you can only sell through an affiliate network (like Clickbank.com or CJ.com) and others you must apply directly with the merchant.

To get started as an affiliate marketer, I recommend signing up for Clickbank.com and CJ.com and seeing which products you would like to promote. Then just contact the merchant and tell them you'd like to be an affiliate (through Clickbank or CJ you just apply on the website, and it's a pretty simple process).

The main ways to get affiliate sales are:

> ➢ Linking to the affiliate product within your blog posts
> (Works great when doing product review posts).

> ➢ Linking to the affiliate product with a banner ad on your sidebar
> (Works great if the offer applies to most of your visitors and you have a good banner or graphic for it. Most merchants will have banner graphics you can use - just ask them.)

> ➢ Linking to the affiliate product in an email to your email list.

These are the best ways to sell affiliate products. There are many others if you're creative, but I recommend starting here. Then focus the rest of your energy on driving traffic to your blog. You'll sell more affiliate products by creating a good blog that attracts more visitors.

3. SPONSORS

There are many ways you can get sponsors for your blog.

SPONSORED POSTS

A sponsored post is where a company or person pays you to write a post on behalf of that company. They might want you to review one of their products, talk about a contest they're running or just mention some of their charity work on your blog.

Sponsored posts can cost anywhere from $10 to $10,000 depending on the size of the blog and its audience, and what the sponsor is willing to pay for that exposure.

To see an example of a sponsored post on one of my blogs, check it out here:

http://bit.ly/VvYfH3

I was paid $150 for that post. It's not life-changing money, but for less than an hour of work, it's worth it. And it builds my credibility because I can now say my site was sponsored in part by Dole.

Disclosure: To abide by FTC laws in the US, make sure you always disclose at the bottom of your post if you were paid or given free product in exchange for writing the post.

SPONSORED PRODUCT LAUNCHES AND ONLINE EVENTS

You can also get sponsors for your site if you are doing a product launch that you expect to reach a large audience.

Events like teleseminars, webinars and livestreams are attractive to sponsors because they allow them to connect with your audience in a more intimate way than through a banner or text advertisement.

BLOG SPONSORSHIP RESOURCES

GLAM Media - has a special program for bloggers for advertising as well as sponsored posts. Learn more at:

http://www.glam.com/

CHAPTER 5

SOCIAL MEDIA MARKETING FOR BLOGGERS

Social media is by far the most effective form of driving targeted traffic that will convert and make you money!

Most people think that Google search traffic is the best for conversion and monetizing your blog. But the simple fact of the matter is this: most of your Google search traffic will come from long-tail keywords. Searches like "How to eat healthy when you're a diabetic" with several words in them that are searched very rarely are called long-tail keywords, and it's search phrases like these that will make up the majority of your search traffic.

Although many of these long-tail keywords will be very focused and convert well, many of them will not. You'll get hits from searches like "corn dog cancer risk bread allergy" which do not convert at all. And that's okay; it's still traffic and you should be grateful for it.

But the Holy Grail of blog marketing and traffic monetization is Social Media. Here's why.

SOCIAL MEDIA IS HIGHLY TARGETED

I wrote a short article on my blog about my recent interview with Dr. Terry Wahls who was in a wheelchair from Multiple Sclerosis, and then 9 months later, after changing her diet, biked 18 miles in one day.

What happened? I shared it on Facebook and got some comments and some decent traffic.

Then... nothing.

Until 4 months later, someone retweeted one of my tweets about it. Then 100 people retweeted it. Then it got picked up on Facebook and received over 15,000 views from Facebook alone in just one week.

Needless to say, I was excited to see that post go viral and my blog get a ton of traffic. But what about converting all that traffic into sales?

Well, from those 15,000 visitors from Facebook, about 500 opted in to my email list. Not bad, huh? To get a similar conversion from advertising would cost at least $500 to $1,000 or more, and wouldn't be nearly as powerful because these people all came to my list from their friends on Facebook. I also made several affiliate sales from those visitors as well! It was a good week for my blog.

This is why social media is so targeted and converts so well, because it is social. When your friend shares something with you, you pay more attention and get more excited about it than when you see an advertisement. It's just human nature.

Not only does social media traffic convert well, it's also free! So you might as well use it.

MARKETING YOUR BLOG ON SOCIAL MEDIA

Here's the system I've used to market my blog on Social media quite effectively.

1. SET UP FACEBOOK COMMENTS

A ton of my traffic comes from the Facebook comments system. I installed it along with the standard Wordpress comments. This gives people more options for leaving comments, and allows me to take advantage of both comment platforms.

I've created a tutorial video for you that will show you how to install Facebook comments on your Wordpress blog in 5 minutes. You can watch the free tutorial here on YouTube:

http://bit.ly/ZveU2T

2. GET SHAREAHOLIC'S PLUGIN

There's a Shareaholic Plugin that embeds sharing buttons for various social networks such as Facebook, Twitter, Pinterest, LinkedIN, Instagram, and more at the bottom or top of each of your posts. Get it! It's awesome.

Download the plugin here:

http://bit.ly/107rNl3

If you don't know how to install Wordpress plugins manually, I created this video to show you how:

http://bit.ly/ZF697w

3. USE TWITTER EFFECTIVELY

I wrote a best-selling Amazon eBook about Twitter marketing that shows you exactly how I use Twitter, spending less than 15 minutes a day on it to get over hundreds of visitors to my blog every month.

Rather than re-hashing all that information for you here, you can get access to all the great Twitter training for free as my gift to you:

http://bit.ly/MlNne2

4. SETUP YOUR FACEBOOK FAN PAGE FOR SUCCESS

Facebook fan pages are one of the best ways to drive consistent traffic for free.

First of all, create your fan page if you haven't already. When you create your page, keep in mind that there are two theories for fan page naming.

1. SIMPLE NAMING

Use your company, blog or personal name. Plain and simple. This helps build your brand and looks the most professional.

2. DESCRIPTIVE NAMING

Descriptive naming is where you name your fan page in a way that will attract attention to what you do. For example, How To Make Money Online With Tom Corson-Knowles[3] is my fan page name.

This way, when you post or when others share your content or mention your fan page, it shows up with your descriptive name, making it more likely for Facebook users to click it, come to your page, and become your fan, opt-in for your free report, or learn more about you.

Descriptive naming is especially powerful if you enjoy commenting, sharing and interacting on Facebook,

---

[333]   The URL can be different – mine is:
https://www.facebook.com/OnlineInternetMarketingHelp

because every time you do so your Fan Page name is being seen by potential customers in their newsfeeds.

For more free Facebook marketing tips, strategies and support, check out my book *Facebook for Business Owners* available on Amazon.

WHICH NAMING STRATEGY SHOULD YOU USE?

I recommend using the simple naming strategy for most businesses.

If you're a very social person and love to comment and interact on Facebook and are building your own personal brand, then it may be better to use the descriptive naming strategy in order to take advantage of all your social activity on Facebook for attracting new customers to you.

CHAPTER 6

HOW TO OUTSOURCE TO GROW YOUR BLOG

At one point, you will realize you've just got so many new opportunities from your blog that you won't have time to manage it all. You will need to bring in help to run the blog and grow it even bigger and faster.

I believe it's a good idea to learn how to outsource your blog before you need to, so you don't get overwhelmed when you get to that point where you *have to* start outsourcing.

There are many aspects of blogging you can outsource, and you don't need to hire a full-time employee right away. You can manage most blogs easily with one or two virtual assistants, and/or a team of guest writers (who will write for you for free as guest bloggers.)

Let me start by sharing with you what I've found to be the most useful, productive and easiest ways to outsource your blogging business: hiring a writer, hiring web designers and technical help, hiring SEO contractors, and hiring a virtual assistant.

HIRING A WRITER

Hiring a blog writer can be a life-saver for any serious blogger, especially if you have a regular publication schedule (You better have a publication schedule by now.)

Once you've hired a writer, it becomes so much easier to manage the blogging business. Instead of you having to write articles every day and every week, you've hired someone to do that for you, and you will need that extra free time to work on other areas of your business to become a successful blogger.

HOW TO HIRE A WRITER

I've tried all kinds of ways to hire writers. I've tried classified ads, social media requests, asking for referrals, and much more.

What I've personally found to be the best way to find high quality writer candidates is to use Craigslist combined with personal referrals.

Why?

Well, first of all Craigslist is free. And free is good.

Second, every time I post a writing job on Craigslist I get at least 10 responses, meaning I have more high quality candidates to choose from. You never want to be stuck making a choice between just 2 or 3 writers because chances are you're not going to be making a good choice when the options are limited.

This is how most new entrepreneurs work: they find one graphic designer, never ask for references or compare prices, hire them, and then wonder why they're broke!

It's because you need to shop around for the best help. Don't just hire your neighbor because you know him. Hire the person who will do the best job on time for the best price. And the only way you can know for sure that you're doing that is to do your research and talk to at least ten potential candidates.

The more candidates you interview, the better chances you have of finding a great writer at a great price. And when I say "interview," you can do all that through email, Skype or phone – it's up to you. I prefer initial interviews over email, and only use phone calls or Skype when necessary. I've never even talked with on the phone or Skype with some of my writers – just by email.

Here's how use Craigslist to find writers. Feel free to R&D (Rip-off and Duplicate) my system!

STEP 1. WHERE TO POST ON CRAIGSLIST

I always post in the San Francisco Writing Gigs section of Craigslist because a) it's free and b) thousands of writers search through it every day. You can find it here:

http://sfbay.craigslist.org/sfc/wrg

You can also post in other cities, but I find the San Francisco Writing Gigs section is often big enough to find enough candidates for the job.

STEP 2. WHAT TO POST

Here's a sample of one of my actual ads I posted to find a writer for my blog. It worked well for me, so I recommend you model it (if not in style, at least in the overall detail that I provide in my ads). Detailed ads are MUCH better because they sift out responses from people who are not qualified or can't do what you want them to do.

Here's the ad:

> *"I'm looking for a health and nutrition writer for my blog, someone who can write very high quality, detailed and well-research link bait articles on various nutrition and health topics. I'll only be needing 1 or 2 such articles a week, each should be 1000-5000 words, depending on whether it's a long list or a shorter myth-buster article.*
>
> *You won't need to ever show up at the office! Just email the written articles in.*

I'm looking for a long-term relationship here as I'll have to teach you my personal style and help you emulate it as well as possible.

Requirements:

Must be familiar with "link baiting" and controversial writing (you can just research link baiting tactics to get a feel for the kinds of articles - lists, mythbusting, common mistakes to avoid, etc. are all good starters)

Must have degree or in-depth knowledge in nutrition or some other health field

Must write well with no typographical errors

Must be willing to develop a long-term relationship (12 months at least)

Must deliver writing on time or ahead of time (I don't mind if you want to write a month's worth of articles in the first week, just please don't go for weeks without anything)

You can check out the blog at http://www.tomcorsonknowles.com/blog"

STEP 3. WHAT YOU MUST INCLUDE IN YOUR AD

Here are what I feel to be the most important elements to include in your ad:

➢ How many articles do you want and how often?

➢ How long should the articles be?

> ➢ Is this a short-term or long-term gig?
> (You'll get better writers if you advertise it as a long-term opportunity for them).

> ➢ How much are you paying?
> (I recommend $10-$20 an article to start – more on that later)

> ➢ What topic(s) do you need the articles to be on?
> (Be specific.)

> ➢ What requirements do you have?
> (List specific requirements like "no typos," "must deliver on time," etc. This helps weed out bad candidates)

Include a link to your blog so that writers can feel you out before contacting you (this could also drive a significant amount of traffic to your site – which is a nice added bonus).

STEP 4. WHAT TO PAY

I recommend you start by paying $10-$20 per article for articles that are at least 500 words.

Now, you might think this is way too low, or too high a price to pay, but I've found this is the "sweet spot" that will get you the best writers at the best price in most situations.

Here's the deal: there are literally millions of good writers out there who need work. And millions of those writers are willing to work for $10 to $20 for a 500-1000 word article.

In fact, this is the standard in the blogging industry. The average writer for the Huffington Post and other big blogs actually gets paid just $5-$10 per article (although they get paid based on their page views which is an entirely different issue. The point is that the average professional staff blogger gets paid just a few dollars per article).

Despite the fact that this is the standard for the blogging industry, you will get writers who respond to your ad complaining that you're not offering enough money for their work. They will complain and beg for you to pay more. When you're just starting out, don't do it!

Why pay $500 for a 500 word article when you can pay $10 for a similar article of similar quality? (I have actually had writers tell me their rate is $500 for a 500 word article!). Honestly, what are they writing that could possibly be worth $500 for 500 words?

But back to business... Blogging *is* a business, and you need to treat it like a business. Don't overpay your writers. Just find a writer who is a good fit and is willing to do the work at a reasonable price.

Once you're raking in cash from your site, you can choose to pay your writers above-average fees if you feel like it. Until then, manage your cash wisely.

A WORD OF CAUTION

There are many writers out there who speak English as a second language or who are just plain bad writers. Needless to say, you should avoid them.

At first, you may find that many writers who are willing to be paid $10-$20 per article fall into the category of bad writers. Just keep looking until you find the good ones. Trust me, there are millions of good writers willing to work for these rates. Just keep reposting your Craigslist ad until you find the right writer for you.

I always ask potential writers to send me one article that I can use for my blog before I agree to hire them. That article is their "application" so to speak. If I like the article, I will post it and pay them and keep them on board. If I don't like the article, I may ask them to edit it if it's a simple remedy, but if the article is just too bad to post, I tell them they're not the right person for the job.

This way I never have to spend money on any articles or writers unless they actually do a good job.

WHEN TO PAY YOUR BLOG WRITERS

When should you pay your writers? Many writers will ask to be paid up-front. Don't do it!

You should never pay a writer upfront for their work. Always pay them after they've delivered their work.

I'm telling you this because I was burned more than once by writers who I paid and then never did what they said they would do. I want to save you the time and money now instead of having you make the same mistakes I did when I first started.

I have my writers send me an invoice once a month and then pay them via Paypal for the work they delivered that month. I recommend you do the same.

A NOTE ABOUT STANDARDS

I have standards in my business. Some might call them rules. One of these rules is that I never pay a writer upfront. Every time I've broken that rule, I lost money in one way or another. That's why I have the rule.

And even though people keep saying the old phrase, "rules are meant to be broken," I've found that every time I break my own rules in business, I lose. So stick to your rules! They're there to protect you.

Another helpful rule I have is that I never hire anyone until I've interviewed at least three people for the job. Whether I'm looking for a web designer, coach, consultant, or writer, I make sure to interview as many people as I can before choosing one. This way I can get a better idea of what the right price is and what kind of experience and talent is available in the marketplace.

HOW TO FIND GUEST BLOGGERS

Another great way to outsource part of your work as a blogger is to accept guest posts on your site. Just as I believe it's a great idea to trade your content for a link back to your site, I also believe it's a great idea to trade a link from your site for content from good guest bloggers.

How do you get guest bloggers to give you content?

I have a simple philosophy for this. First of all, if someone wants to guest blog on my site, they have to contact me. I'm not going to waste my time trying to convince a blogger to write a guest post for my site because a) there are millions of bloggers who want a link from my site and b) I could write an article faster than the time it would take to convince someone to write an article for my site in most cases.

HOW TO FIND GUEST BLOGGERS

You can post on MyBlogGuest to let people know that you're accepting guest posts for your site:

http://myblogguest.com

I also recommend creating a "Guest Blogging Guidelines" page for your site. This page should have all the information a potential guest blogger would need in order to submit an acceptable article to you. I also recommend linking to your Guest Blogging Guidelines page from your Contact page. That way, hopefully instead of emailing you, potential guest bloggers will first see your guidelines and then contact you once they know your guidelines, saving you time.

You can see my blog's Guest Blogging Guidelines as a sample here:

http://bit.ly/WBLOIL

HOW TO DECIDE WHETHER OR NOT TO ACCEPT A GUEST POST

I generally have guest bloggers email me the article directly so that I can review it personally.

If I don't like the article or don't think my readers will like it, I reject it.

I also check every potential article on Copyscape[4] to make sure it's not plagiarized or duplicate content. Google will penalize your website if you post duplicate articles, so I always try to make sure that my articles are 100% unique (Although 90% or better is okay).

You will need to pay about 5 cents per article using Copyscape's Premium service in order to see whether the article being sent to you is unique or not, but trust me, it's 5 cents well spent!

Obviously, if someone sends me a plagiarized article or duplicate article, I reject it. If it's because they're a new blogger and didn't know any better, I'll ask them to write me a unique article and resubmit it to me. Otherwise, I just won't work with that person.

HIRING WEB DESIGNERS AND TECHNICAL HELP

When it comes to hiring a web designer or someone to help you with the technical aspects of your site, I always like to get at least three quotes for any major

---

[4] http://copyscape.com/

work and always have at least three contractors whom I can call anytime to get work done.

You see, the problem with most entrepreneurs online is that they only have one web designer. This is all great and fine until he gets sick, leaves the country or decides not to return your emails.

I've actually seen entrepreneurs running six-figure online businesses who were slaves to their one web designer. When he was around doing work, everything was great! When he wasn't, the business fell apart because no new web pages or design changes could be made.

Look, this is YOUR business and YOU need to be in control of it. This means firing any web designers who are too slow or don't do the job right. You should always have a backup person to do the work you need done when you need it done.

You can find a web designer on Craigslist as well in the "Computer Gigs" section. You can also find them on sites like Elance, Vworker, ODesk and Freelancer.

Always remember this: get at least 3 quotes for projects, and have at least 3 people you can call to get your work done. Don't be a slave to your web designer or freelancers!

OUTSOURCING LINK BUILDING AND GUEST POSTING

Once you've done guest posting for a few months yourself and understand how it works, you'll have enough knowledge and education to be able to intelligently outsource guest blogging and link building for your site if you choose to.

In general, you should expect to pay $15-$50 to hire a writer who will write a unique article for you on your general topic and submit it to high quality sites in your niche.

Basically how I do it is this:

First, I let my writer know what keywords I want in the anchor text of the links. I give her a list of about 10 keywords and tell her to use them randomly. It's important to mix up the anchor text in your guest posts, otherwise Google would get suspicious if you have 100 links to your site and every single one has the exact same anchor text like "Weight loss." Google would see that as spammy, and rightfully so.

I have my writer find the potential sites to guest post on and tell her which sites I'd love a link from and which sites I reject using the criteria I shared with you before about PageRank, AlexaRank and the site's design and content. Then, my writer writes articles and submits them to those sites.

Every month, she sends me an invoice listing the published guest posts and I review them and pay her $25 per post.

Why pay her $25 and my other writers only $10-$20? Well, she earns it! She has to find the sites, contact them, build the relationships, write the article, submit the article and take care of all that hassle for me. All that time she spends doing that is time saved for me, so it's worth it.

Of course, you can always try to negotiate a better deal, or hire a full-time assistant who can work more cheaply or effectively for you.

DON'T LISTEN TO SEO "GURUS"

Many SEO gurus or blogs out there will tell you that you can buy backlinks from places like Fiverr.com to boost your traffic.

I can't recommend highly enough that you do not buy links <u>ever</u>.

I have personally seen my websites de-indexed by Google from buying backlinks from Fiverr. That $5 gig that looked too good to be true ended up costing me thousands of dollars. I don't want that to happen to you!

That's why I never recommend buying backlinks from Fiverr or anywhere else. It's just not worth it.

Never buy links. Period. It's bad business.

HIRING SEO CONTRACTORS

Honestly, I don't even recommend hiring an SEO contractor until you have a very good working knowledge of Search Engine Optimization and understand how it's going to help your business. If anything, I recommend you hire a decent writer who you can teach my Guest Blogging System to, and have them go implement this system for you like I mentioned before.

HIRING VIRTUAL ASSISTANTS

Virtual assistants (VAs) are basically contractors who do any of the managerial and administrative work you don't want to. You can have your VA do everything from SEO to writing to cleaning out your email inbox.

Here are the most useful tasks I've found for my VA to help me grow my blogging business:

> - Find blogs in my niche and contact them on my behalf (using the Guest Blogging System)
> - Managing my Facebook fan page daily posts
> - Transcribing videos and interviews
> - Social bookmarking and forum marketing
> - Other mundane or repetitive tasks

THE OUTSOURCING MANAGEMENT SYSTEM

Now that you understand how outsourcing can help you grow your business, let's talk about how to do it right.

You see, just hiring someone from Craigslist and telling them to post some cool pictures on your fan page once or twice a day isn't good enough. You need to give your contractors very clear guidelines and a checklist of the tasks they need to complete.

I've found checklists to be the most effective way to communicate with contractors and make sure they do the right things at the right time, and that there are no miscommunication.

Furthermore, having a checklist makes it much easier for you should you need to find a new contractor to take over the work of a previous contractor who for whatever reason can't do the job anymore. The biggest problem in the contracting/outsourcing business is turnover, so you need to make sure you have a system for managing that change. Otherwise, you might end up wasting your time teaching the same basic tasks over and over to a new contractor every few months. Instead, just write down the key steps in a checklist, and systemize your business.

In short, having a checklist for any contracted work means that you have systemized that work and that anyone can do it for you, anytime, when given the system.

Instead of making you struggle to create your own checklist, I've created a checklist template for you that you can use for all your contracted work. Of course, you'll have to put the specific directions for your business but it will give you the starting point.

You can download your free outsourcing sample checklists here:

http://bit.ly/XBLvUi

CHAPTER 7

WHY MOST BLOGGERS FAIL – AND WHY YOU WON'T

When you first start blogging, making progress can feel slow. It does take time to see results. You have to have patience. Even once you implement my guest blogging system that I shared with you in Chapter 2, it's going to take time for that traffic to build up to your site to where readers are flocking to your blog.

Here are some things you have to understand about the process so that you can stick with it even when it looks like not much is happening in the first few months.

THE GOOGLE SANDBOX

There are many reasons for the time lag between link building, and posting content, and when the traffic starts coming in droves. The main reason is Google's "Sandbox." Google's algorithm penalizes new sites when it comes to search engine rankings. This helps Google reward long-term websites and avoid a lot of problems with new spam sites accidentally ranking too highly in search engines.

The problem is, of course, that you want more traffic to your blog and you want it now. You don't want to wait 6 months for Google to start giving you a good bit of credit for your links and high quality content.

But here's the deal: you just have to be patient. You can't change Google's algorithm. You can't cheat the system. You have to work with the system if you want to succeed.

As Warren Buffet says, *"You can't have a baby in 1 month by getting 9 women pregnant."*

It takes consistent posting and patience to become successful as a blogger. That doesn't mean you just sit on the computer watching your stats, hoping for new readers to come by any minute. It means you do the work you know you should be doing consistently, and then you go enjoy your life while you wait for the results to come.

Trust me, when you implement the guest blogging system, the results *will* come. It'll just take a few months before you get out of the Google Sandbox.

WORK THE SYSTEM

You just have to let the system work and not focus on your results for the first six months. See, if I had been focusing on my results when I started my Tom Corson-Knowles blog, I would have quit 3 or 4 months in because I was only getting 2,000 to 3,000 hits a month on my site, a very disappointing number for the hours of effort and energy I was putting in.

But I stuck to it because I knew about Google's sandbox. I knew that I was going for the long-term rewards of blogging, not just a short-term, overnight quick buck. I wanted to build a profitable, lasting business, not some fly-by-night get-rich-quick scheme.

And after 9 months, I was getting over 100,000 hits a month on the site. But I didn't change anything about what I was doing. I was still building links by guest blogging and posting regular content on the site.

What I'm saying is that even though my activity did not change, my results changed dramatically, because the activity was starting to pay off when Google took my site out of the sandbox.

Always remember that if you want to build long-term success and wealth, you must focus on adding more value to your customers (readers), and continue to execute on the fundamentals of your business. When it comes to blogging, those fundamentals are providing high quality content and building high quality links, which you've already learned how to do in earlier chapters.

What I'm saying is that all you need to do is focus on the fundamentals and have patience. The system works, if you work the system.

Don't give up too early. It's the #1 reason most bloggers fail to create a sustainable business.

CHAPTER 8

TIME MANAGEMENT AND PRODUCTIVITY FOR BLOGGERS

One of the biggest challenges most bloggers have is how to manage their time. You've got your publication schedule to keep up with, reader comments to respond to, research for new article ideas, guest posting to keep up with, writers and contractors you have to manage, and lots of emails as well.

With so many moving parts to the business of blogging, it's no wonder most bloggers fail to keep up and succeed. But there is a way to manage it all, and succeed in spite of the workload. I'm not going to sugarcoat it and tell you that you can get rich blogging without doing any work. That's ridiculous!

If you want to be a great blogger, it's going to take an investment of time, energy, effort and a little bit of money. All true success in life requires a serious investment.

Since you've read this far already, I know you understand that you don't need to spend a lot of money on SEO, web design or automated software, so you're already way ahead of 99% of bloggers out there who don't know what you know about the guest blogging system, how to set up your own blog and why you should avoid "magic button" software and sleazy internet marketer sales videos.

So, first of all, congratulate yourself on how far you've come already! What you've learned already in this book will save you the years of time it took me to learn just these few principles about blogging.

But what you need now isn't just more knowledge and how-to advice on blogging. What you need is a system to manage your own time so that you can implement what you've already learned in this book.

Wouldn't it be great if you woke up in the morning and knew EXACTLY what you were going to be doing that day for your business? How would you feel knowing that you already knew what to do each day and you knew how to do it and you knew WHEN you would do it?

You see, most people fail at time management not because they want to, but because they get stuck in old habits of doing things that no longer serve them.

I'm going to teach you the system that I've used, and hundreds of my students have used, to better manage their time each day. This system is what has allowed me to build my business so quickly. I know it will work for you too.

THE 5 STEP TIME MANAGEMENT SYSTEM FOR BLOGGERS

Time management is much more than just taking some seminar or learning some system. It requires daily and weekly maintenance, and the right mindset to help you get what you want in life.

Here's the system I've used to dramatically improve my life and my productivity. It will help you as well if you apply it consistently.

STEP 1. DECIDE WHAT YOU WANT

You've probably heard this before, but I can't even begin to tell you how important it is to your success. Most people live their entire lives trying to get what *other* people think they should want.

We go to school to become a doctor because that's what our parents wanted.

We marry the wrong person because we think that's what society expects of us.

We get a job instead of starting our own business because it's "the safe thing to do."

We spend hours a day watching TV and checking Facebook because we "don't want to miss out" on what everyone else is doing.

I'm telling you right now: you must stop doing what other people want you to do.

Don't even do what I want you to do!

Only do what you want to do. This is the key to success in life – in *your* life.

Write down right now in your notes...

What do you really want in your life?

When you know what you really want, and you're not afraid to go after it, no one can stop you from achieving your goals.

STEP 2. SCHEDULE THINKING TIME

One of my mentors, Keith Cunningham, is ridiculously rich. His net worth is more than $100 Million.

Keith told me that the key to his success was scheduling "Thinking Time" on a regular basis.

I said, "What the heck is thinking time, Keith?"

He said, "Thinking time is when I schedule time to sit down all alone, by myself, without any distractions, and think about my life and my business."

Keith went on to share with me how exactly he "thinks" during thinking time.

FIRST, SCHEDULE YOUR THINKING TIME

You must write down in your calendar each week exactly WHEN you will do your thinking.

SECOND, ASK THE RIGHT QUESTIONS

During your thinking time, you should have a pen, a notebook, and a list of questions to ask yourself. Here are some of my favorite questions, some I learned from Keith, and some are my own:

> ➤ *What can I do today to improve my situation?*
>
> ➤ *What don't I see? What risks are there that could do damage to my business or my life?*
>
> ➤ *What can I do today to increase my income?*
>
> ➤ *If there was one person I could talk to and get advice from to improve my life, who would that be? How can I get in touch with that person?*
>
> ➤ *Are there any activities or time-wasters I can eliminate from my life right now?*

THIRD, ANSWER THE QUESTIONS

The magic of thinking time, as you will soon discover for yourself, is that *you already know what you should be doing to grow your business and improve your life.*

You don't need a spiritual guru or a blogging genius to tell you what your next steps should be. Does learning help? Of course it does.

But the problem is not that you don't know enough to succeed in business; *the problem is that you don't do what you already know you should do!*

This is why thinking time is so valuable. Your mind will start coming up with all kinds of amazing ideas for how you can improve your life and your business. Just let the ideas flow in your journal or notebook.

Trust me, you'll have better ideas about how to improve your business than 99% of the people you know. All you have to do is harness those ideas and act on them.

FOURTH, IMPLEMENT YOUR IDEAS

After your thinking time is over, you'll have a list of things to do. Now go do them!

I always keep my list by my bed at night, and just before bed I review it and add any new ideas I come up with.

In the morning, I take my list to my computer and I start on the most important tasks first.

I guarantee that if you do this regularly and keep it up, you will see dramatic improvements in your life and your business.

That's all there is to using Thinking Time to grow your business.

STEP 3. ELIMINATE DISTRACTIONS

Now that you've decided what you want and you've scheduled regular thinking time, it's time to get rid of distractions that are stealing your time and ruining your business (and possibly your personal life as well.)

The average American watches 4 hours of TV a day (that's over 28 hours a week.)

I guarantee you that anyone can build a successful blog working 28 hours a week, and earn a great income from it.

You see, the problem isn't that there are not enough hours in the day for you to succeed; it's that you're not using the hours you have in the best possible way.

Now I'm not saying you're doing a horrible job. Heck, I don't even know you personally yet. But I do know this: we all self-sabotage. We all have bad habits. We all have internal obstacles that we need to overcome in order to achieve more in life.

So I'm going to list some common distractions that waste people's time and keep them broke. And then I'm going to encourage you to schedule your own "thinking time" to discover what distractions have been coming up for you recently, and how you're going to eliminate them once and for all.

COMMON DISTRACTIONS AND TIME WASTERS:

> ➤ Television

> ➤ Email (especially newsletters, spam, chain letters and chit-chat)

> ➤ Social Media (Hey, social media marketing is great, but looking at all your friends' pictures on Facebook can get out of hand quickly)

> ➤ Surfing the web

> ➤ Reading the news (Trust me, if it's truly important news, your friends, family or business partners will tell you about it)

> ➤ Hanging out with negative friends

> ➤ Commuting to work (listen to educational CD's in your car so that you can learn to earn more while you drive)

CREATE YOUR OWN "ELIMINATING DISTRACTIONS PLAN"

Schedule 30 minutes to an hour to think about what distractions have been wasting your time recently. Can't afford an extra 30 minutes? Then you *really* need to do this right away!

If you can't afford 30 minutes to plan how to overcome distractions then I guarantee the distractions have already taken up so much of your daily time that you will never succeed until you get rid of them.

So for your own sake, schedule 30 minutes right now to work on this. If in those 30 minutes you discover how to save yourself just 1 minute a week, it will have been a worthy investment. Of course, most people who do this exercise don't just save 1 minute a week; they often save several hours a week!

STEP 4. SCHEDULE LEARNING TIME

Abe Lincoln is known for his famous quote:

> *"Give me six hours to chop down a tree, and I'll spend the first four hours sharpening my axe."*

You see, Honest Abe knew that the absolute best use of one's time in life is to spend time preparing and learning how to do something better so that you can get the job done much faster.

The same is true for blogging. If you become a better writer, a better business person, a better blogger, and a better internet marketer, you will naturally and automatically get more work done and achieve more success in less time.

I recommend scheduling at least 30 minutes a day to learn. Whether you want to read books like this one, listen to audio trainings, watch video training courses, or go to live seminars, events and workshops is up to you. But the key is that you schedule time to learn more so that you can earn more.

It's as simple as that.

STEP 5. SCHEDULE WORK TIME

This one is probably the most obvious of all, but it's also very important. Make sure you schedule your work time. When you run your own business it's much different than being an employee.

You have to schedule your own work time and motivate yourself to get it done. You can't rely on anyone else to tell you what to do or make you get it done. It's all up to you.

What gets scheduled gets done. So schedule your work, and work your schedule.

TIME MANAGEMENT

Always remember the five keys of time management:

1. Decide what you want

2. Schedule thinking time

3. Eliminate distractions

4. Schedule learning time

5. Schedule Work Time

If you do these 5 things, you will be far ahead of 99% of bloggers.

CHAPTER 9

SUPER SECRET BLOGGING TIPS AND TRICKS

Now I'm going to share with you a handful of blogging tips and tricks that are quick and easy to implement and will help set you apart from the competition immediately.

1. CREATE YOUR OWN BLOG DIRECTORY

This tip alone has given me many high quality backlinks to my site with very little effort other than setting up one page on my blog.

Here's how it works.

Blog directories are a great way to build links. But most bloggers actively try to find other blog directories, and rarely think of creating their own.

I'm a bit of a maverick, so I decided to start my own blog directory. One day, I just had the idea to create a new page on my blog. I called it my "Nutrition Blog Directory," and then provided instructions for visitors to get a listing in my blog directory.

The requirement is you have to link to my blog to be listed in my directory.

I actually get several visitors a day to my sites when they search for things like "health blog directory," "internet marketing blog directory," etc.

You can even create multiple pages on your site with blog directories within your blog. The sky is the limit. I would just recommend keeping them in your niche. For example, my internet marketing blog directory is listed on my internet marketing site, not on my health related site.

You can see my blog directories here and model your own after them:

Feel free to R&D (Rip off and duplicate) my blog directories:

Nutrition Blog Directory:

http://bit.ly/VETa1h

Internet Marketing Blog Directory:

http://bit.ly/UQtY7b

Just make sure you have unique content on each of those pages so that Google won't penalize you for duplicate content. You want your directories to be found by people searching in Google.

2. PODCASTING

Podcasting is like internet radio. A Podcast show is a radio show that is streamed through the internet and is available for download on iTunes.

Podcasting can be a great way to drive traffic to your blog, build your e-mail list, connect with your readers and potential customers, and build relationships in your industry. I've used my podcast shows to land interviews with some of the top experts in the world in my industry, and you can too!

Just saying that you are the host and founder of a show sets you apart from most other bloggers out there, and it can give you access to key resources and connections that can help you grow your business.

NINJA PODCASTING TIP

Interview experts in your industry on your Podcast show to build your credibility. You can have experts begging for you to interview them by simply posting a query on HelpAReporter.com stating that you are looking for experts to interview for your show.

You can also get sponsors for your Podcast show. But that's a whole different topic.

You can create a podcast show for free and have it on iTunes by the end of the week. I use and recommend Podomatic for beginners. You can sign up for Podomatic here (it's free to get started until you need more bandwidth):

www.podomatic.com

If you have a little more technical know-how, you can create a podcast show and host it on your own blog using Wordpress like I do for my Publishing Profits Podcast show at:

www.publishingprofitspodcast.com

3. REPURPOSE YOUR CONTENT

Repurposing content can dramatically increase your and profits with very little extra work.

Repurposing content is basically taking content from one place (like your blog) and publishing it somewhere else or in another form (like in a YouTube video).

For example, you could record a video and post it to YouTube. Then, you could repurpose that video by stripping the visuals, converting it to an audio file and posting it on your podcast show (or you could just post it on your podcast as a video podcast).

Then, you could further repurpose that content by having someone transcribe the video and posting the transcription on your blog as an article.

Then, you could further repurpose that content by packaging several of your blog articles and turning them into an eBook, which you could then sell on Amazon, Smashwords or another ebook site. Or you could just give it away for free as an incentive for people to sign up for your email list.

Because there are so many ways to publish content online, the sky is the limit when it comes to repurposing content. And yes, this is a reliable, ethical and legitimate strategy.

Think about it this way: some people prefer to read, some prefer to listen on their iPod, and some prefer to watch video. So if you're not providing your readers (customers) with the content they want in the format they want it, then you're missing out and so are your customers. You owe it to them to give them what they want, and what they want is your content in the form that's easiest for them to consume.

Repurposing your content is a sure-fire strategy for dramatically increasing your reach online, and helping a lot more people with your information.

All successful bloggers understand repurposing. Many of the most successful bloggers received book deals because of their blogs. So they went from blog to book.

Other bloggers create training programs or ebooks that they sell. Where did the content come from? It came from old blog posts they repurposed and updated and turned into an ebook or course.

Once you've created content on your blog you'll find there are many other ways to help people (and make a profit) from that content.

THANK YOU
FOR READING

I want to thank you personally for taking the time to read this book. Did you know studies show 90% of people who buy a book never read it and finish it?

The fact that you've read to this point makes you in the top 10% of people. You are a star. You are a winner!

I can't thank you enough for your commitment to yourself to be great and to become a successful blogger. Blogging will give you the potential to reach millions of people with your message. I trust that you are now ready for this power.

Go out and make it happen!

If you ever have any questions whatsoever about how to implement this material, feel free to email me personally with any of your questions at:

www.tckpublishing.com/contact

To your success,

Tom Corson-Knowles

P.S. I wanted to include some bonus material for you. Whether you're a brand new blogger or experienced, I hope the bonus resources on the following pages will help take away any last stumbling blocks that could stop you from becoming a blogging success.

Now go out there and put this information into action today.

BONUS RESOURCES

BLOG STARTUP ACTION GUIDE

This action guide will give you everything you need to know to get your blog going in the right direction. Just follow these simple steps along with the daily action guide below and you will start to see results.

1. Create your self-hosted Wordpress blog (Visit www.BlogBusinessSchool.com for the free training on how to start your own self-hosted blog in 15 minutes)

2. Create a Facebook Fan Page for your blog at:
    wwwfacebook.com/pages

3. Create a Twitter Account for your blog:
    www.twitter.com

4. Create a Pinterest Account:
    www.pinterest.com

5. Get TweetAdder:

    http://bit.ly/NAVZ0s

6. Get Feedburner:

    www.feedburner.com

7. Start writing posts and implementing the guest blogging system

8. Install recommended Wordpress plugins (see the chapter Top 10 WordPress Plugins For Bloggers)

9. Create a blog publication schedule and stick to it

DAILY BLOG ACTIVITIES CHECKLIST

This checklist will give you a daily guide of some of the most important activities for growing your blogging business. At first, you will likely want to do all of this yourself. Once you understand how everything works and fits together, you can start to outsource some or even all of these daily activities.

Write a blog post or article (15-60 minutes, depending on length, writing speed, etc.)

This article can be for your own blog or you can use it as a guest blogger

FACEBOOK

Post or schedule 3 updates on your fan page. At least one of these posts should be a photo. Respond to all comments and messages.

TWITTER

Schedule at least 20 Tweets for the day. If you're using TweetAdder, you can just write new Tweets once a week or so.

Check your mentions and direct messages on Twitter and reply to any relevant conversations.

RELATIONSHIP BUILDING

Contact at least 5 other bloggers asking them to collaborate through guest blogging, social media or something else.

COMMUNITY BUILDING

Respond to any comments on your own blog and try to be as helpful as possible with any questions people ask.

TOP 10 WORDPRESS PLUGINS FOR BLOGGERS

Here's a list of my top plugins for blogging. I highly recommend using each of these plugins to help you get more traffic and manage your blog easier.

1. Pinterest Plugin adds a Pinterest "Pin It" button to every image on your site.

   http://www.wordpresspinterestplugin.com/

2. Akismet blocks spam comments.

   http://www.akismet.com/

3. All in One SEO Pack helps with basic on-site SEO for your blog.

   http://www.wordpress.org/extend/plugins/all-in-one-seo-pack

4. The Official Facebook Plugin allows you to easily and quickly install Facebook comments, like buttons, recommended posts and much more. It's

the official Facebook plugin for Wordpress and works great.

http://www.wordpress.org/extend/plugins/
facebook

5. Fast Secure Contact Form allows you to create a contact form super easily and quickly in Wordpress and install it on any page or post in your site you want to. Every blog should have a contact page. I can't tell you how many opportunities and checks I've received because I had a contact page that made it easy for others to reach me from my blog.

http://www.wordpress.org/extend/plugins/
si-contact-form

6. Google XML Sitemap for Videos is a great sitemap for Videos. Helps increase your SEO results if you post videos.

http://www.wordpress.org/extend/plugins/
xml-sitemaps-for-videos

7. Google XML Sitemaps is a great sitemap for Google indexing. It helps increase your search engine traffic.

http://www.wordpress.org/extend/plugins/googl
e-sitemap-generator

8. Jetpack Lite gives you nice and easy Wordpress stats within your Wordpress dashboard so that you can track your traffic easily without having to login to Google Analytics every day.

http://www.wordpress.org/extend/plugins/
jetpack-lite

9. Post Layout is an awesome plugin. It allows you to add any html, text, pictures, links or anything else you want before, in the middle of, or after every post on your site. I use it to add an opt-in box below my blog posts.

http://www.wordpress.org/extend/plugins/
post-layout

10. Shareaholic is a plugin that adds share buttons below or above your blog posts. It's great for getting more social traffic.

http://www.wordpress.org/extend/plugins/
sexybookmarks

11. TweetMeme Retweet Button is a great Twitter button for your blog with a simple counter. It gets a lot of action so I recommend putting it at the top of your blog posts.

http://www.wordpress.org/extend/plugins/
tweetmeme

BLOGGING RESOURCES AND TOOLS

Here I'm going to list many of the other resources and tools I use to support my online business.

GoDaddy is what I use to buy domain names (for example, www.blogbusinessschool.com). I love their 24-hours customer service which is a must whenever you have technical problems.

http://bit.ly/13e9KYa

BlueHost is a hosting service for your website. If you want to build your own blog using Wordpress you will need hosting. They also have great 24-hour customer service which I really appreciate when I need help.

http://www.bluehost.com/track/tcorsonk

Aweber is an email autoresponder service. With it, you can create web forms on your site so that people can sign up for your email list automatically by simply filling in their name and email.

I recommend Aweber because it's a cost effective, reliable autoresponder and email list management service.

http://aweber.com/?375818

Easy Webinar Plugin is a plugin for Wordpress that allows you to create a beautiful evergreen webinar to sell products or services or just to educate your audience. You can get a free trial which allows you to create one custom webinar with custom landing pages and the webinar will run every day if you want it to. It's great for anyone who's selling products online.

http://a5969g13i6yfrvb31ql9ku5r45.hop.
clickbank.net/?tid=BOOK

Optimize Press is a great Theme for Wordpress which allows you to build custom squeeze pages and sales pages. It will save you a lot of money compared to hiring a web designer every time you need to make a new squeeze page.

http://nanacast.com/vp/97647/39530

TweetAdder is some awesome software for automating your Twitter tweets and a lot of other cool things. This tools saves me hours of work every day.

http://www.tweetadder.com/idevaffiliate/
idevaffiliate.php?id=15532_0_1_6

Chris Farrell Membership Site is an amazing training site for online marketers to learn how to make money online. Chris is one of my mentors and his information and training has been priceless for me.

http://juicetom.farrell10.hop.clickbank.net

EXCERPT FROM *FACEBOOK FOR BUSINESS OWNERS*

FACEBOOK MARKETING STRATEGY

For most small businesses, making money with Facebook requires building the right system.

Unless you have a brand like Coca-Cola with billions of people around the world who consume your product regularly and pretty much everyone in the world knows who you are, you have to create a system that will allow you to capture new leads and turn those leads into customers.

You can't afford just to "advertise" on Facebook without actually generating leads and sales because you'll run out of money advertising sooner or later if you're not generating sales.

The bad news is you'll have to develop a system that makes Facebook profitable. The good news is it's much easier than you think!

All you have to do is set up a "marketing funnel" on Facebook where you get your fans and prospects to request more information and then you build the relationship and turn your fans into paying customers.

HOW TO CREATE A SALES FUNNEL

For those of you who understand online marketing and building a sales funnel, this will be super easy. If you're not familiar with building a sales funnel, then it'll be a little bit of a learning curve but I think you'll find it incredibly intuitive and easy to understand.

A sales funnel is basically the system or series of steps your prospects must go through in order to become a paying customer.

Figure 1 - Sales Funnel

STEP 1. TRAFFIC

Above is a diagram of a simplified sales funnel. At the top of the funnel we have a very broad segment of prospects – for example, all of your Facebook fans, or, even broader, everyone who sees your Fan Page.

HOW DO YOU GET TRAFFIC ON FACEBOOK?

There are many ways to get traffic including using Facebook ads, posting regular status updates, interacting on Facebook, and building your fan base through your other websites and in your stores. We'll talk about how to use Facebook Ads in the next chapter.

REGULAR STATUS UPDATES

Posting regular status updates (at least one or two a day) is the easiest and most effective way to attract new fans and keep your old fans coming back for more. It's also free! Even if you spend millions of dollars on ads, no one cares if you don't post regular status updates so make sure you do that.

GET FANS FROM YOUR WEBSITE

If you have a website make sure you put a Facebook Like Box on the sidebar of your site so that your visitors can like your fan page with one click.

You can get a Like Box here from Facebook:

https://developers.facebook.com/docs/
reference/plugins/like-box/

I also recommend you use Facebook Comments on your website and the Facebook like button for your web pages. If you use Wordpress, you can simply install the Facebook For Wordpress Plugin:

https://developers.facebook.com/wordpress/

If you don't use Wordpress for your site, then you can have your webmaster install Facebook comments for you.

INTERACTING ON FACEBOOK

If you love sharing and social media or are just naturally an outgoing person then you can attract new fans by joining conversations on Facebook. You can join groups, help answer questions on other fan pages and share new ideas with others in your industry.

If you're going to use this strategy, make sure to use Facebook as your fan page rather than as your personal profile so that when people see your posts, they see it was written by your fan page and can then like your page.

To do that, simply click the tiny arrow at the top right of the screen next the home button and pick which fan page you would like to use Facebook as.

But we know just because someone visits our fan page doesn't mean they're going to buy from us right now. So what we do is send them to a lead capture page or "squeeze page" as many online marketers call it.

On your lead capture page you ask for the prospects' name and email address so they can get more information about you and your products (and so you can market to them on a regular basis).

Here's an example of one of my lead capture pages if you've never seen one:

http://www.blogbusinessschool.com/

Generally, you want to offer something that your potential customers will see as very valuable and you want to offer it for free in return for your prospect's name and email. Examples of free products include a sample, an eBook, a training video or series of videos or a free consultation, just to name a few. Offering something for free does several good things for your business.

First, it will dramatically increase the number of new leads you get.

Second, it will increase goodwill with your prospects because they will be happy they got something valuable for free.

Third, it deepens your relationship with your prospects because they get to experience your free product before they make the decision to become a paying customer.

You can create your own Capture Pages and landing pages on Facebook using the Static Iframe app (it's free):

https://apps.facebook.com/iframehost/

You will need to know basic html to build a landing page on Facebook or have your web designer do it. Alternatively, you can redirect traffic from your Facebook landing page to one of your website landing pages. To do that, just click "redirect" once you've set up your iFrame tab.

STEP 3. MAKE OR DELIVER YOUR OFFER

After the prospect opts in to your email list for more information, it's now time to either deliver the information you promised or to make an offer to buy one of your products.

Often, online marketers will make what's called a "one time offer" (OTO) immediately after a prospect opts in. In this one time offer, you might offer your product at a discount or a bundle package at a discount. OTOs are especially effective when using advertising because the immediate sales generate by an OTO can either offset the costs of your advertising or completely pay for the cost of the ads.

STEP 4. FOLLOW UP, FOLLOW UP, FOLLOW UP

"Follow up, follow up, follow up until they buy... or die!"

~ Tom Hopkins

Once they've opted in to your email list, they can either buy from you or unsubscribe – because you're going to continually follow up with them as long as they give you permission to!

If someone opts in to your email list it means they have at least some interest in your products and services so it's your job to help them get what they want.

Depending on your business, you may want to follow up with these prospects with a new email once a week, once a day or once a month.

THAT'S IT!

That's really all there is to building a sales funnel – at least the basics of it. Once you've got your sales funnel set up and capturing leads and following up with them you will start to see REAL SALES being generated from Facebook. Without a funnel, it's very difficult to monetize Facebook and make it profitable.

[End of Excerpt] If you enjoyed reading this section of *Facebook For Business Owners*, you can grab your copy here:

http://amzn.to/ZEjXcz

SPECIAL FACEBOOK GROUP

Come join our Facebook group just for authors like you who want to network, share ideas, collaborate and connect with other like-minded authors. In this group we'll be sharing our successes, marketing tips and strategies with each other so that we can all continue to succeed as authors.

www.facebook.com/groups/KindlePublishers

CONNECT WITH TOM

Thank you so much for taking the time to read this book. I'm excited for you to start your path to creating the life of your dreams as a Kindle author.

If you have any questions of any kind, feel free to contact me at:

www.tckpublishing.com/contact

You can follow me on Twitter:

www.twitter.com/juicetom

And connect with me on Facebook:

www.tckpublishing.com/facebook

You can check out my publishing blog for the latest updates here:

www.tckpublishing.com/

I'm wishing you the best of health, happiness and success!

Here's to you!

Tom Corson-Knowles

ABOUT THE AUTHOR

TOM CORSON-KNOWLES is the #1 Amazon best-selling author of *The Kindle Publishing Bible* and *How To Make Money With Twitter*, among others. He lives in Kapaa, Hawaii. Tom loves educating and inspiring other entrepreneurs to succeed and live their dreams.

Learn more at:

http://amazon.com/author/business

Get the free Kindle publishing and marketing video training series from Tom here:

http://www.ebookpublishingschool.com

OTHER BOOKS BY
TOM CORSON-KNOWLES

Destroy Your Distractions

Email Marketing Mastery

The Book Marketing Bible: 39 Proven Ways to Build Your Author Platform and Promote Your Books on a Budget

Schedule Your Success: How to Master the One Key Habit That Will Transform Every Area of Your Life

You Can't Cheat Success!: How The Little Things You Think Aren't Important Are The Most Important of All

Guest Blogging Goldmine

Rules of the Rich: 28 Proven Strategies for Creating a Healthy, Wealthy and Happy Life and Escaping the Rat Race Once and for All

Systemize, Automate, Delegate: How to Grow a Business While Traveling, on Vacation and Taking Time Off

The Kindle Publishing Bible: How To Sell More Kindle ebooks On Amazon

The Kindle Writing Bible: How To Write a Bestselling Nonfiction Book From Start To Finish

The Kindle Formatting Bible: How To Format Your Ebook For Kindle Using Microsoft Word

How To Make Money With Twitter

101 Ways To Start A Business For Less Than $1,000

Facebook For Business Owners: Facebook Marketing For Fan Page Owners and Small Businesses

How To Reduce Your Debt Overnight: A Simple System To Eliminate Credit Card And Consumer Debt

The Network Marketing Manual: Work From Home And Get Rich In Direct Sales

Dr. Corson's Top 5 Nutrition Tips

The Vertical Gardening Guidebook: How To Create Beautiful Vertical Gardens, Container Gardens and Aeroponic Vertical Tower Gardens at Home

INDEX

www.ingramcontent.com/pod-product-compliance
Lightning Source LLC
Chambersburg PA
CBHW070834070326
40690CB00009B/1547